Wingless I Watch

Emma Woodford

First published 2025 by The Hedgehog Poetry Press

Published in the UK by
The Hedgehog Poetry Press
Coppack House, 5
Churchill Avenue
Clevedon
BS21 6QW

www.hedgehogpress.co.uk

ISBN: 978-1-916830-19-6

Copyright © Emma Woodford 2025

The right of Emma Woodford to be identified as the author of this work has been asserted in accordance with the Copyright, Designs and Patents Act 1988.

All rights reserved. No part of this publication may be reproduced, stored in or introduced into a retrieval system, or transmitted in any form, or by any means (electronic, mechanical, photocopying, recording or otherwise) without prior written permissions of the publisher. Any person who does any unauthorised act in relation to this publication may be liable for criminal prosecution and civil claims for damages,

9 8 7 6 5 4 3 2 1

A CIP Catalogue record for this book is available from the British Library.

For Guido and l'Espérance

Contents

Haiku 7
Gulls 8
Puffins 9
How I became Milton's Cormorant 10
Sea Raven Black 11
Sea Dreams 12
Fulmars 13
The Guillemot Question 14
Nazca Booby 15
Manx Shearwaters on Skomer, 1994 16
Gannet 17
Sea Duck 18
Albatross 19
Great Auk 20
Ghazal for Seabirds 21

Acknowledgements 24

Haiku

Seabirds call us here
they know paradise is lost
one fish at a time

Gulls

Glaucous gulls siren around boats,
black backs stride on ancient lava beds.
Aligned with opal skies and cliff tops
lesser black back parents protect
chicks raised on the edge whose cries
reach my bed. I wonder how far
I would follow gulls out to sea.
I lie awake, my intestines a knot
of bladder wrack, twisted
by my incapacity to fly.

Puffins

Pumped puffins click beaks
with mates returning to the burrow.
Soot coloured chicks grow despite
piratic skuas hounding parents
on every homebound catch.

Summer marks the end of colour,
the parading cult of clowns
feel their beaks turn grey.
Testicles shrink to poppy seeds,
female feet skip ocean waves
disappearing into winter out at sea.

How I became Milton's Cormorant

Sat like a cormorant; yet not true life
Thereby regained, but sat devising death
To them who lived;

  Milton, *Paradise Lost, Book IV*

Proud of our pterosaur descent my mate
would dive for bottom lurking fish.
Together we glistened black,
our wings akimbo on the river bank.
Did you know that in China, cormorant chicks
are gagged, trained with tofu to fetch fish,
and sleep wrapped in cotton wool.
Whole villages depend on their survival.
When ring pulls turned my mate's stomach white,
I fled her corpse and Satan flexed my wings
against this slate sky. He gave me a pier from which
I watch your skin wrinkle in the waves and wonder
what loss of innocence I will devise,
what torture will you not survive.

Sea Raven Black

Green back, blue back, black
sea ravens own riverbanks
Green back, blue back, black

Sea Dreams

I see a salt tailed fulmar
trust her tubenose
to smell the way home.

Home is a cushion
of sorrel and thrift
head under wing to sleep.

Waves lap around my bed
I drift on cushions and wish
my fulmar dreams
would carry you away.

Fulmars

Fulmar plumage paid croft rents
Fulmar fat cured toothache and boils
Fulmar flesh was eaten with porridge
Fulmar oil lit lighthouses
Fulmars fly free

The Guillemot Question

How can you not know how guillemots die.

We the chocolate birds who watch
for albatross who hunt our chicks,
raised to fledge on death drop cliffs.

With our uncrushable skulls we dive
to depths unknown to you, beyond
your plastic layers and submarines.

How can you not
know how we die.

Nazca Booby

Parents go fishing out to sea. Chicks in white fluffy coats
lure babies into gangs. My violence addicted eyes
watch bloody skin and feathers fly around nests built on bones.
The pain of my first rip is theirs, blacked out in his bed,
as he came again and again. Frozen cries of avian rape
fill the colony, like when I cried, mother, through ocean mist.

Manx Shearwaters on Skomer, 1994

Dots on a gentle heave, shearwaters
raft at sea waiting for the cover of night.
Silence crashes the sound of waves
on blackened rocks I hope
we are not sitting in the way.
Clumsy birds land head over hurtle.
The ringer catches them one by one,
and reads their lives in numbers.
A giant tucked under his arm,
named BB7233, has flown
from South America to breed.
The bird makes me feel
as if our lives could be written on a ring.

Gannet

You are a chick raised above the rip tide
on a bloody bed in a fishbone nest,
built on shit-stained rocks.

Your parent's sex life started
with an affectionate bite to the jugular.
One hundred thousand gannets
taught you barbed beaks tear to flimsy.

Through locked bills,
threshed wings and wrestled necks
you tiptoed over tsunamis of flesh,
found space to escape
the eternal fight for freedom.

Sea Duck

Ripple my feathers
nibble the imperfections
in his duck curved neck

Albatross

Birds born in the wind

                      wind born in birds

    waltz around the world.

Birds die in wind

                            winds die in birds who

by the end of their magnificent lives

                          have flown millions of fathomless miles.

Great Auk

"No fact in the history of the world is so startling as the wide and repeated extermination of its inhabitants."

Charles Darwin, from Beagle, Patagonia

They say your call was louder than a gannet's
more immense than any bird we had seen
black, white, flightless and downy soft.
We made you genocide pets,
an eccentric walked you in Copenhagen Park.
We set upon your kingdoms from Morocco to the Baltics
from Scotland and South Wales to Labrador and Maine.
We found French cave paintings of you fighting.
We revered you and ate you.
In the famine formed fisheries of treeless Newfoundland
Breton sailors burnt your oil to casserole your sister.
We gathered your eggs
Fabergé bejeweled one for the Queen of England.
We colonized your colonies, extinction carved
memories in granite cliffs.
We are buried with your bones.

Ghazal for Seabirds

Freed from form I'd fly skywards with seabirds
twist, leap and turn with waves of feathery birds.

Foxtrot with fulmars on Viking winds across wild seas,
we'd dance together of love and revelry birds.

Gannet beaks sting salt scratches on my skin and yet
their twisted fishing dives form a lovely bird.

My human heart hears how glaucous gulls cry at night
come be free they call me dream reverie birds.

Chinese cormorants fish so a village can eat,
Milton's devil took the form of lecherous birds.

Knowledge rumbles like foam shoots across a ship's deck
puffin mothers urge young to hide from deathly birds.

When will you know where guillemots go to die sir,
chocolate coated bundles of sweet mystery birds.

Darwin saw how we came, do we know where we go,
to auk-like extinctions for every free bird.

I wish I was an albatross born in the wind,
wingless I watch from clifftops. Cry treachery birds.

Acknowledgements

"Great Auk" was published in Quarter(ly) Journal, 2023.

This collection of poems was long listed for the Aryamati PoetryPrize in 2023 and the Cinnamon Pamphlet Competition 2024.

Wingless I Watch is written in *response* to Adam Nicholson's inspirational book 'The Seabird's Cry'

It is a good idea to read this with Cantus Arcticus playing in the background.

These poems would not have reached where they are now without the feedback of the Esperance Writing Group, Jacqueline Saphra and Arji Manuelpillai who all helped to slice them open so I could put them back together again.

www.ingramcontent.com/pod-product-compliance
Lightning Source LLC
Chambersburg PA
CBHW030313100526
44590CB00012B/631